T

"Kay Adshead s angry stripped-down s— pt bleeds h— —ty ...solo performer Noma Dumezweni is mesmerising in the spotlight... Words in Adshead's hands are bullets. Brace yourself and see this play – preferably with Jack Straw strapped in beside you"

The Independent

"So meticulously well done, so superbly performed by Noma Dumezweni and so manifestly based on the indefensible facts about what is happening in British detention centres now, that even the most dedicated reactionary would find if difficult to turn away in indifference. This a beautifully crafted work, designed to make British people feel sick with shame at what is being done in our name; and by God it succeeds"

The Scotsman

"Adshead's words are fragile and beautiful, angry and raw ...Dumezweni is magnificent as the frightened but raging bogus woman. She instantly grabs our attention and won't let go. pounding the stage full of disbelief and grief. If anything car confront the idea of refugees reclining in state run hostels wi n pashmina carpets and gold leaf wallpaper, *The Bogus Woman* can"

The List

"a compelling and gut-wrenching indictment of The British Asylum System...Adshead's text is scrupulously detailed and unapologetically campaigning...Noma Dumezweni's performance is as irresistible and demanding of answers as the script itself. Political theatre at its best"

Scotland on Sunday

"Home Office Ministers and civil servants should be nailed to Traverse seats and made to watch this one"

The Herald

D1081028

"Stunningly performed by Noma Dumezweni…a powerful, passionate committed piece of theatre that if seen widely enough might change hearts and minds. If I were Greg Dyke, I would put it on straight on BBC TV and invite Jack Straw to respond in the course of a properly focused rational debate"

Michael Billington/The Guardian

"You don't often hear people crying in the theatre. But you do during *The Bogus Woman.* Kay Adshead's play is a body blow …delivered with top-velocity grace by Noma Dumezweni"

The Observer

"Kay Adshead's powerful asylum drama is a breath of fresh air in a theatrical climate which seem to have forgotten about accomplished agit-prop"

Financial Times

"Beautifully performed with dignified puzzlement and anger by Noma Dumezweni…hammers at the door of our collective complacency about the treatment of asylum seekers in the UK"

Time Out

Kay Adshead

THE BOGUS WOMAN

OBERON BOOKS
LONDON

First published in 2001 by Oberon Books Ltd.
(incorporating Absolute Classics)
521 Caledonian Road, London N7 9RH
Tel: 020 7607 3637 / Fax: 020 7607 3629

e-mail: oberon.books@btinternet.com

Copyright © Kay Adshead 2001

Kay Adshead is hereby identified as author of this play in accordance with section 77 of the Copyright, Designs and Patents Act 1988. The author has asserted her moral rights.

All rights whatsoever in this play are strictly reserved and application for performance etc. should be made before commencement of rehearsal to Peters, Fraser and Dunlop Ltd, Drury House, 34-43 Russell Street, London WC2B 5HA. No performance may be given unless a licence has been obtained, and no alterations may be made in the title or the text of the play without the author's prior written consent.

This book is sold subject to the condition that it shall not by way of trade or otherwise be circulated without the publisher's consent in any form of binding or cover other than that in which it is published and without a similar condition including this condition being imposed on any subsequent purchaser.

A catalogue record for this book is available from the British Library.

ISBN: 1 84002 209 4

Cover design: Andrzej Klimowski

Typography: Richard Doust

Printed in Great Britain by Antony Rowe Ltd, Reading.

for
Raffles

Contents

ABOUT THE RED ROOM

The Red Room was launched in October 1995 by Lisa Goldman and Emma Schad to develop high quality new plays with a critical and original take on the world we live in. Starting life with the creation of a new pub theatre space above the Lion and Unicorn in Kentish Town, and now a production company, The Red Room actively seeks out collaborations with writers and other artists whose work engages with social flux from a radical perspective to make theatre which is complex and critical. The Red Room has increasingly defined its role as a provocateur on the London new writing scene, pro-actively commissioning and developing political new writing. The primary aim of the Red Room's work is to impact on wider society, to develop consciousness or understanding, to challenge accepted ideas about public issues.

RED ROOM PRODUCTIONS

The Traverse/The Bush
2000/01 *The Bogus Woman* – dir. Lisa Goldman
NFT1 – London Film Festival
2000 *My Sky is Big* 35mm short film dir. Lisa Goldman
BAC
1999 *Leave to Remain* by Leon London dir. Lisa Goldman
1998 *Made in England* by Parv Bancil dir. Lisa Goldman
also Watermans, The Bull, Etcetera
1998 *Seeing Red* **a two month festival of dissent**:
Know Your Rights by Judy Upton; *Election Night in the Yard* by Roddy McDevitt; *Its my Party* by Aidan Healy; *The Cows are Mad* by Jon Tomkins; *The Head Invents, The Heart Discovers* by Peter Barnes; *On the Couch with Enoch* by Tanika Gupta; *The Mandelson Files* by Paul Sirett; *The (Bogus) People's Poem* by Kay Adshead; *The Big Idea* by Helen Kelly; *The Ballad of Bony Lairt* by Rony Fraser Munro; *Made in England* by Parv Bancil; *Slow Drift* by Rebecca Prichard; *Thanks Mum* by David Eldridge; *Les Evenements* by James MacDonald; *Stick Stack Stock* by Dona Daley

I wish I'd seen that – Time Out Critics Choice seasons:
1997 *Obsession* by Rob Young dir. Lisa Goldman
1997 *Surfing* by Rob Young dir. Lisa Goldman
1996 *Sunspots* by Judy Upton dir. Lisa Goldman

Royal Court Duke of York and New Ambassadors
1997 *The Censor* by and dir. Anthony Neilson

Assembly Rooms, Edinburgh
1997 *Surfing* by Rob Young dir. Lisa Goldman

Finborough – The Big Story – season about the media
1997 *The Censor* by and dir. Anthony Neilson
1997 *Surfing* by Rob Young dir. Lisa Goldman
1997 *People on the River* by Judy Upton dir. Lisa Goldman
1997 *Tuscon* by Lisa Perotti dir. Janet Gordon

The Red Room Theatre
1996 *Sunspots* by Judy Upton dir. Lisa Goldman
1996 *White Unto Harvest* by Mavis Howard dir. Lisa Goldman
1996 *Creamy* by Leon London dir. Sarah Franckom
1996 *Bacillus* by Kay Adshead dir. Orit Azaz
1996 *Stealing Souls* by Judy Upton dir. Shabnam Shabaze
1996 *The Lottery Ticket* by Roddy McDevitt dir. Yvonne McDevitt
1996 *The Body Trade* by Deborah Lavin dir. Lisa Goldman
1996 *Liar Liar* by Ned Cox dir. Lisa Goldman
1995 *The Night before Christmas* by and dir. Anthony Nielson
1995 *Shuttle* by and dir. Joseph Crilly
1995 *The Shorewatchers' House* by Judy Upton dir. Lisa Goldman

Awards
2000 Fringe First Award – *The Bogus Woman*
1997 Time Out Award – Best Fringe Play
1997 Writers Guild Award – Best Play – *The Censor*
1997 Guinness Ingenuity Award – The Big Story Season
1996 Guinness Ingenuity Award – Coming to Land Season

Mama Quillo Productions

Artistic Directors: Kay Adshead, Lucinda Gane.

It was a widely held belief in the 1990's that when it came to new writing for the theatre, the decade belonged to the lads.

Without doubt, the most squandered resource in British theatre is the talent of actresses over 40.

It is an astonishing fact that in the year 2001, throughout the UK, there are no more female theatre directors than in 1975.

Mama Quillo is a production company for theatre, radio, TV and film, created by women – for men and women.

The Bogus Woman is Mama Quillo's first co-production. In 2001/2, Mama Quillo will produce a new play by Kay Adshead for five women and one man.

The Bogus Woman

Lisa Goldman

The first immigration laws were passed in 1905 to keep out people like my great-grandparents, Jews fleeing pogroms or poverty in eastern Europe. We are all descended from migrants. Yet during the twentieth century the scale of state effort to keep people off this cold, grey island has escalated to an unprecedented level. Now that legitimate migration to the UK is virtually impossible unless you are rich or under the terms of the 1951 UN Convention, a refugee, the New Labour government has systematically targeted "bogus" asylum seekers, scapegoating people for their suffering. The press have had a field day and the indigenous victims of government cutbacks in housing and other social provision have been duped into believing that asylum seekers are to blame. According to a recent MORI poll, 80% of the British population perceived immigrants to be a "drain on national resources."

In such a hostile political climate Kay Adshead's *The Bogus Woman* is a courageous play. Proudly partisan, it takes the side of "the young woman", an African asylum seeker, against New Labour and moreover successfully persuades the audience to take her side too. When Ian Shuttleworth for the *Financial Times* said the production was "perversely, a breath of fresh air in a theatrical climate which seems to have forgotten about accomplished agit-prop", he pointed to a greater truth.

What theatre lacks at the moment is public vision and daring. Agit-prop is still perceived as "preaching to the converted" whereas in fact *The Bogus Woman* is revelatory – it informs and challenges us about issues not seriously debated in the press. On the other hand, mainstream theatre does "preach to the converted" when it explores public issues. Unsurprisingly it tends to reflect the dominant ideology of social inclusion, official anti-racism, meritocracy, and other New Labour hypocrisies. Material, progressive change is as feared by our current "enlightened" establishment as those that preceded it.

I would like to thank those enlightened producers who had the artistic vision and/or political conviction to enable this play to reach an audience. First and foremost Tom Morris at BAC who gave The Red Room Studio 1 in 1998 for two months for our 16 short plays about Blair's Britain, *Seeing Red*, sight unseen. One play was Kay's embryonic version of *The Bogus Woman*; thanks too to Waterman's Arts Centre who allowed us to "try out" a work-in-progress version of the full length play two years on; special thanks to the Traverse Theatre for having the guts to offer us a gig when no new writing theatre in London would. Finally, big thanks to Mike Bradwell of the Bush for knowing a good show when he sees it and for sharing in our excitement.

I would love to see all artists and programmers fight for provocative and progressive agendas but I am also aware that most would rather not look beyond their cosy theatres to the angry frightened inmates of Campsfield Detention Centre. Making theatre for social change is certainly a more challenging, interesting and worthwhile endeavour than promoting theatre as a lifestyle choice, a divertissement before dinner for the middle classes. I hope that *The Bogus Woman* may give others the courage to pro-actively commission work that critically addresses public issues.

I hope that this script is widely read and performed, perhaps by huge casts in schools or community groups, that it leads people to get involved in making things better. I hope that one day there will be no need for a play like *The Bogus Woman*, that there will be no border controls left, here or anywhere. Meanwhile, Kay's play is an example to us all, to open our eyes to what is being done in our name and to have the courage to stand up and say that it is wrong.

Lisa Goldman
London, 2001

Author's Note

I knew about the work of The Medical Foundation for the Care of Victims of Torture. Coincidentally, at the same time as Lisa Goldman asked me to write a short piece for the Red Room's *Seeing Red* season at BAC, I attended one of their awareness-raising events. At about the same time, I saw the dramatic protest on TV of the detainees at Campsfield.

For the short piece that I wrote for the Red Room, I read hundreds of stories of refugees seeking asylum in this country; the Refugee Council provided me with some of the source material. All of these were sad, but some were sickening, so horrifying as to be almost unreadable. "Inspired" by these terrible stories, I created my story of *The Bogus Woman*. It is more shocking than some and less shocking than others.

I researched Campsfield with the help of the Campaign to Close Campsfield in Oxford. They put me in touch with a young man who was detained in Campsfield at the time of the protest and was unfortunate enough to be one of the nine black men charged with causing riot and affray, who became known as the Campsfield Nine. My research was partly in the aftermath of the protest and the draconian measures then pursued, and in the run up to the trial. There are so many different stories that come out of the protest that the transcript of the trial of the Campsfield Nine was indispensable in giving me an insight into the events. Throughout the process of research, I simply could not believe what I was hearing. I could not believe that the violation of human rights of vulnerable people was happening in England in 1997 (outside Oxford no less) and more shocking still in the first year under a Labour government for which I had waited 18 years! I wrote my play before xenophobia hit the headlines. I have written it because I hope it will give people an insight into what it can really be like to seek asylum in this country. I also hope it may change minds.

Kay Adshead
London, 2001

Commissioned by The Red Room, *The Bogus Woman* was first performed as a work in progress at Waterman's Arts Centre on 29 June 2000. Premiered at the Traverse Theatre on 4 August 2000. Subsequently performed at The Bush Theatre on 7 February 2001, with the following cast:

YOUNG WOMAN, Noma Dumezweni

Director, Lisa Goldman

Designer, Ti Green

Lighting, Simon Macer-Wright

Sound, Jules Shapter

A large aircraft landing.

Airport ambience.

Lights snap up.

YOUNG BLACK WOMAN, made up and in a pretty cotton frock with a hold-all, stands.

YOUNG WOMAN:
No, no,
up, up,
not down,
not here,
she's not here,
no one's here.
Go up
back up to the clouds,
up to Anele!

But it's cold,
colder than here,
she'll need the shawl.

Frantically she empties the bag looking for the shawl.

My mother made it,
from white spit
and silver hair,
and ivory years.

I must go back up to the clouds
back up to my people.

(*Sharply.*) Don't tell me what to do!
Take your hand off my arm!

Yes I have a passport.
I don't know,
in my bag.

I..., I...
I don't know my name.

(*Quickly.*) You heard me.

I don't know which flight
I can't remember.
I don't know
where from,
you tell me.

No, I have no family
in England.

(*Quicker still, the words spilling out.*) I told you in my bag!
I told you in my bag!

No I'm not on holiday!

No I've no one meeting me!

No I'm not staying with friends!

I don't know yet!

Does it matter?

Does it matter?

Lights change.

England is a
rectangle
above my head,
out of the corner
of my eye,
a small grey rectangle
of sky.

The days have congealed
into a grey viscous lump,
into a week.

And then, there are
the questions.

YOUNG WOMAN AS ENGLISH IMMIGRATION
OFFICIAL:
You still claim
not to know
which organisation
the "soldiers"…came from
specifically.

YOUNG WOMAN:
No.

YOUNG WOMAN AS ENGLISH IMMIGRATION
OFFICIAL:
They *were* soldiers were they?

YOUNG WOMAN:
Yes.
I don't know.

YOUNG WOMAN AS ENGLISH IMMIGRATION
OFFICIAL:
They wore uniforms?

YOUNG WOMAN:
Yes. Partly.

YOUNG WOMAN AS ENGLISH IMMIGRATION
OFFICIAL:
Partly?

YOUNG WOMAN:
Yes…partly.

YOUNG WOMAN AS ENGLISH IMMIGRATION
OFFICIAL:
You're sure they weren't
neighbours
for instance?

YOUNG WOMAN:
(*Laughs.*) They weren't neighbours.

YOUNG WOMAN AS ENGLISH IMMIGRATION
OFFICIAL:
They were not known to you personally?

YOUNG WOMAN:
They were not known to me personally

YOUNG WOMAN AS ENGLISH IMMIGRATION
OFFICIAL:
There is no record of you
having worked as a journalist
on the paper you mentioned

YOUNG WOMAN:
(*Beginning to get agitated.*)
I worked for eight and a half months,
three days a week

YOUNG WOMAN AS ENGLISH IMMIGRATION
OFFICIAL:
Perhaps you've given us the wrong dates?

YOUNG WOMAN:
I've given you the right dates

YOUNG WOMAN AS ENGLISH IMMIGRATION
OFFICIAL:
And you say it's as a direct consequence
of articles written by you
that the "atrocity"
was committed

YOUNG WOMAN:
That and other things.

YOUNG WOMAN AS ENGLISH IMMIGRATION
OFFICIAL:
What other things?

YOUNG WOMAN:
(*More agitated.*) I've told you

look at my statements
look at your files.
You'll see my words
fucking words,
fucking…

Lights change.

A different white square room

YOUNG WOMAN AS FIRST INTERROGATOR:
Where did you get your papers?

YOUNG WOMAN:
I can't tell you that

YOUNG WOMAN AS SECOND INTERROGATOR:
You realise
you have committed an offence
entering the country
with a false passport?

YOUNG WOMAN:
Yes

YOUNG WOMAN AS FIRST INTERROGATOR:
A serious offence!

YOUNG WOMAN:
I was in fear of my life.

YOUNG WOMAN AS FIRST INTERROGATOR:
So far
we can find no evidence
to substantiate
that claim.

YOUNG WOMAN laughs.

YOUNG WOMAN AS SECOND INTERROGATOR:
That's a nice dress
you're wearing.

YOUNG WOMAN:
(*Laughs.*) Is it?

YOUNG WOMAN AS SECOND INTERROGATOR:
You have American make-up
in your bag
and five hundred pounds.

YOUNG WOMAN:
(*Confused.*) Have I?

My friends gave it to me.
Yes. My friends.

YOUNG WOMAN AS SECOND INTERROGATOR:
(*Triumphant.*) It says here you have a sister studying
fashion drawing
in London…
Perhaps you came over
to see her

Slight pause.

have a holiday

Slight pause.

do a bit of seasonal shopping

Slight pause.

see the sights

Slight pause.

and then stay on

Slight pause.

just a few weeks

Slight pause.

or a few months.

YOUNG WOMAN:
  (*Quietly.*) She never made it to England,
  my sister –
  because she's dead.

  (*Knocking over the chair.*) You fucking
  fish-faced
  English cunts.

  She's dead!

  Pause.

  I am taken to another
  square room
  with a high window.

  Two men in short white coats
  restrain me
  one pulling my badly mended
  broken arm
  rough as shit.

YOUNG WOMAN AS NURSE:
  Well, you shouldn't be
  such a silly girl.

YOUNG WOMAN:
  The other sticks his needle
  in me.
  They can't make me sleep.
  In bed
  I watch the small
  grey rectangle of England,
  the veins of English cloud,
  and weep.

  I pace –
  pick up a magazine
  or two,
  flick through.

Pause.

The very page
the very frock
bright blood red
my sister Abo drew
and coloured in
the very line
she smudged
with a small wet finger

I can hear
her laugh

Lights change.

I was spoken to
in my country
at passport control
and spoke back

exactly as rehearsed,
my voice as thin and sharp
as an actress.

At the airport
in the mirror
and with a start
I caught sight
of the small painted girl
with staring eyes
who is playing me.

Yes – a holiday
two or three weeks.

My husband's up to his eyes
in work
do a bit of shopping
see the sights –

no family as such
but friends…
of friends…
of friends.

Sudden dazzling light.

Up the ramp
I feel my ancestors
hot breath on my face
hear their hearts pump
and all the old songs

*The plane musak turns into ancient African music; this plays
throughout the scene.*

The plane has a voice too
it whispers like a young lover

and holds me tight
too tight.

Cloud minutes

I first saw my husband
in bright sunlight

throw a chuckling tot
at the air,
so high,
that for a split second
the baby seemed to float
or fly.

My mother said
she fell for my father
one carnival night
under a sliced moon
when he bandaged her foot
after kissing each toe.

Music builds.

At the point of death
the sharp blue point
my grandmother cradled my grandfather
crooning
before letting go
she said
of all the years
and watching them float
up
like a child's balloon.

She speaks more quickly.

Cloud minutes are centuries
that suddenly part
and
through a hole in the sky,
the bird dead fly,
our ancestors,
my grandmother's, grandfather's
people.

Spirits
tapping at the window
with their strong beaks
and cawing

Anele
Anele

I am going in the plane
To Anele
and Yemi
and Abo
and mother
and father.

And Anele
with blue black eyes
smiles and

reaches out to me
with one small
brown
dimpled
hand

African music suddenly climaxes and then dips.

Yes
I'm the vegetarian
Thank you.

No, no,
I'm quite alright
just a bit hot.

Thank you,
yes
I've flown before.
Something to take my mind?
Yes.
Thank you.
Thank you.

A magazine
in English

Tall white women
in chain mail dresses
and flag-faces –
red white and blue.

England's
turning the pages
Yemi told me,
turned on its head

England spins on the other side
of the clouds
holding out
its one good hand

an old hand

holding out
its one good
hand to me.

(*Astonished.*) Campsfield Detention Centre.

A tangled tower
of twenty foot high razor wire
secretly coils all the way
from Oxford

(*Very anxious.*) Where am I?

How long will I be here?
What happens next?
What happens now?

YOUNG WOMAN AS GUARD:
Shut up
little nigger woman

YOUNG WOMAN:
(*Whispers.*) Group 4
Prison for Profit
wardens
ex army
hired to brutalise
in twelve-hour shifts
at four pounds an hour

YOUNG WOMAN AS FELLOW DETAINEE:
Don't catch his eye girl
he's in a mood today.
He spilt his coffee
down his best shirt
see?

YOUNG WOMAN AS GUARD:
What are you whispering about?

YOUNG WOMAN:
...I need a change of clothes.

YOUNG WOMAN AS GUARD:
Yeah...
and I need
a new set of wheels
darling.

YOUNG WOMAN:
Is it possible to go to the field today?

YOUNG WOMAN AS GUARD:
No.

YOUNG WOMAN:
Why?

YOUNG WOMAN AS GUARD:
Drainage problems!

YOUNG WOMAN:
Still?

YOUNG WOMAN AS GUARD:
Drainage problems!

YOUNG WOMAN:
Can I have the key to the library?

YOUNG WOMAN AS GUARD:
No.

YOUNG WOMAN:
How do I complain?

YOUNG WOMAN AS GUARD:
You don't.

YOUNG WOMAN AS FELLOW DETAINEE:
Complain
and they transfer you to another jail

without appeal.
Ban visitors.
Intercept your calls.
Lose your files.
Send you back.
I'm telling you girl
keep your head down.

YOUNG WOMAN AS GUARD:
And your fat nose out.

YOUNG WOMAN:
A boy arrives
perhaps sixteen?
A child man
with troubled eyes –
and shaking hands.

YOUNG WOMAN AS GUARD:
Take your thumb
out your face hole, son!

YOUNG WOMAN:
The boy moans
his soft mouth
bubbling groans.

The flame
in his eyes
lights
the blue touch paper
of my mother's heart.

(*To BOY in some distress.*) Don't cry.
Let me hold you.
There little brother
see

She wraps her arms around herself.

You're safe.
You're safe
with me.

YOUNG WOMAN AS WARDEN:
(*Quietly.*) Eh snooty kex
mits off!

Back off!
Do you hear me?

Screams.

Stand up
and back

There's no room
for social interaction
of that sort
in here

Turn a blind,
and
we'd have
enough
little black monkeys
in a blinking,
to sink
all Kidlington.

YOUNG WOMAN:
For the first time
in twenty five days
the child-man speaks.

YOUNG WOMAN AS CHILD-MAN:
(*A hoarse whisper.*) Excuse me

YOUNG WOMAN AS GUARD:
Yeah?

YOUNG WOMAN AS CHILD-MAN:
    I request
    a full medical examination
    and for my file
    to be put on record.

YOUNG WOMAN AS GUARD:
    Request
    refused.

YOUNG WOMAN:
    For me
    however

YOUNG WOMAN AS DOCTOR:
    Would you mind undressing?
    Down to bra and pants
    please?
    Behind the screen

YOUNG WOMAN:
    Yes

YOUNG WOMAN AS DOCTOR:
    Thank you

YOUNG WOMAN:
    Did you hear me?
    Yes
    I would mind.
    I was given
    a complete physical examination
    shortly after arriving at Heathrow,

    another four weeks later
    another fourteen days ago.
    I found the last doctor's
    questions
    invasive and upsetting,
    his manner rude and brusque.

    There was no third party present.

YOUNG WOMAN AS DOCTOR:
(*Softly.*) Back in your country
you were raped
it says

YOUNG WOMAN:
That's right

YOUNG WOMAN AS DOCTOR:
This is new information
to us

YOUNG WOMAN:
Is it?

YOUNG WOMAN AS DOCTOR:
It must have occurred to you
you might be pregnant

YOUNG WOMAN:
I am not pregnant

YOUNG WOMAN AS DOCTOR:
I see

YOUNG WOMAN:
I miscarried early

YOUNG WOMAN AS DOCTOR:
It says in your notes
you had a baby,
not miscarried

YOUNG WOMAN:
I had a baby
then miscarried.
I was raped
the day
after giving birth
to my husband's child.

YOUNG WOMAN AS DOCTOR:
Really?
And you got pregnant?

YOUNG WOMAN:
Yes I got pregnant
then miscarried.
God has been good to me.
Not your God.

Lights change, very dim.

YOUNG WOMAN AS FIRST FRIEND:
You must eat.

They speak softly, kindly, anxious.

YOUNG WOMAN:
My husband's friend
a day after
what happened.

YOUNG WOMAN AS FIRST FRIEND:
Ice cream
a small spoonful
see
it won't hurt your mouth.

YOUNG WOMAN AS SECOND FRIEND:
And drink,
you must drink.

Green tea,
hot and sweet
and barky.

YOUNG WOMAN AS FIRST FRIEND:
Remember
our last party
sitting on the terrace?

I slipped
and tripped
and smashed
the blue teapot.

Can you remember?

YOUNG WOMAN:
Tragedy
has opened up
a chasm
between us.

Nobody
dare look
anybody
in the eye.

The music
of pain
is silence
and shame.

I can't remember
hearing
the ticking of a clock
in their warm kitchen
before.

I am taken
to a back door
in the city.

Down a thousand
stone cold steps
to a warm damp hole.
There's already a blanket there
a bucket smells of shit
and someone's hat.

A newspaper

She laughs.

A newspaper
on every yellow page
letters small and faint
strangely unfamiliar
and sly
e's and p's and i's
make words
fucking words
fucking…

She starts to whimper.

YOUNG WOMAN AS SECOND FRIEND:
Sssh!

Frantic whispers.

You mustn't make
a sound
you put our friends
at risk

Not a cough
not a sigh

I'm sorry
it's such a terrible place.
I'll try and come
every day
with food.

Try and sleep.

YOUNG WOMAN:
I dream
I'm suckling
an old grey grinning bull
with a gold tooth

and a diamond stud.
And I feel myself
drain slowly away.
It is not an unpleasant
dream.

Awake on the third day
my milk comes through.

My breasts bite
and I burn up.
As directed,
I express
into the shit bucket,
first the lactose
then the warm white watery milk,

taking each breast
in two hands
and pumping.

One night,
mad with waking dreams
I suck from my own breasts
hoping to taste Anele
and my old sweet life.

I taste death,
too sweet
and warm
and I vomit.

In the fourth week
alone, still,
after a particularly long
bout of painful cramp,
sitting up from the bucket
I see a tiny foetus
grinning in the puke and piss.
I cover it with

the newspaper,
with the grinning yellowy words
and turn away.

Lights change.

YOUNG WOMAN AS FEMALE GROUP 4 GUARD:
I can tell
a Ghanaian
right –

from a Gambian,

a Kenyan
from a Nigerian,
a Somalian
from an Angolan

At twenty,
thirty,
forty feet
at least.

YOUNG WOMAN:
Chatty Caryn
one of the Group 4
lady guards
boasts of her
observational expertise.

YOUNG WOMAN AS FEMALE GUARD:
Not by the boat race
that is a hopeless case
but by the bum.

You mark my words,
the nearer the equator
that you get,
the higher
ride the buttocks
by and large.

Hit the Congo
and you can eat
your breakfast
off the bastard's
fat backside.

Now
Iraqis
are quite different
to Pakis.

YOUNG WOMAN:
Two hundred souls
did I tell you?
Broken
or breaking
in Campsfield
England.

YOUNG WOMAN AS FEMALE GUARD:
Iraqis
like to have
a little shout,
a run about.

It takes
a plate
of curried eggs

to prise
a Paki
out his gaf
so you can
dust about.

Eh lazy puss?
Eh?
Do you hear me?
Eh?

YOUNG WOMAN:
>An older woman
>with a perforated ear drum
>and three fingers missing
>told to get up off her fat arse
>spits
>and is made
>to clean the toilets.

YOUNG WOMAN AS CHILD-MAN:
>Excuse me sir?

YOUNG WOMAN:
>The child-man
>still afraid
>of shadows
>after three sleepless nights
>complains politely
>about the noise

>coming from
>the Group 4 Rec room
>again,
>and discovers
>the next morning
>his phone card
>magically mislaid!

>As for me
>I still wear
>the same clothes.

YOUNG WOMAN AS SOLICITOR:
>Good morning again!

YOUNG WOMAN:
>I have a legal representative
>now, Mr Pennington,
>trying to be cheerful,

hard pressed
with troubles of his own.

YOUNG WOMAN AS SOLICITOR:
You're looking well.

YOUNG WOMAN:
My eyes are yellow
and my skin is grey.

YOUNG WOMAN AS SOLICITOR:
Goodness,
more notes for me.

YOUNG WOMAN:
He's smart
in a good
grey suit
but
a button's missing
from
his left shirt cuff.

His wife has cancer.

He coughs,
and shyly
from his wallet
takes a snap

of a large boned lady
in a pretty hat

weeding

in an English
country garden,

smiling and sensible.

They met
at University

YOUNG WOMAN AS SOLICITOR:
The chemo's
knocking
her for six
poor pet

but she expects
to make a full recovery.

YOUNG WOMAN:
A full recovery.

As for me

YOUNG WOMAN AS SOLICITOR:
The problem stays the same.
We can't convince anyone
your life's in danger.
I've got the letter from your brother here…

YOUNG WOMAN:
My brother
wrote to the British Government

telling them if I returned

on my arrival
I would almost certainly
be taken away
for questioning
and incarcerated
before being shot

(*Softly.*) or worse.

YOUNG WOMAN AS SOLICITOR:
That's all very well
and it's all good stuff
but to be honest
it won't cut mustard
with the powers that be…

Anyone could have written it

And again
there's the big problem
and I'm sorry to tell you,
after all this
the newspaper
still refuses to verify your claim
that you worked there
as a journalist
for eight and a half months
three days a week.

YOUNG WOMAN:
I snatch his papers,
shuffle through,
then stare –

It's the wrong newspaper
Of course!

The difference in the title is one word
one dangerous word.
Despite being most careful
in my instructions
all these months
the English authorities
have been writing
to the wrong fucking paper.

Lights change.

*YOUNG WOMAN takes the shawl, drapes it around herself
and strikes a pose.*

YOUNG WOMAN:
(*Laughs.*) What do you think?

I audition
for the latest Broadway hit

escape
and make it big?
Not quite!

The Agent
comes to the warm hole
at the dead of night,
and brings false papers
at a price.

He smiles.

but stands well back.
The lice
jump in my hair

My lips infected.
I lick the yellow ooze
I'm hungry now
is it a miracle?

YOUNG WOMAN AS AGENT:
You'll have to fix her up!
She stinks.
And then

a dress
a coat
and shoes.

You'll have to cut your hair.
Naomi Campbell's had it short,
that's the trend,
remind me to bring scissors
when I come back,
we don't want other
passengers to complain.
You'll have to smile,
a bit of blusher
won't hurt

My wife's got some old make up somewhere

American mascara
lipstick
shadow, gloss
I'll hunt it out.

You're a pretty girl.
Cheer up.
We'll do you up
like one of the top models
in the mags

Tape: African drums.

YOUNG WOMAN AS IMMIGRATION OFFICER:
The Asylum Division is not satisfied that the applicant
qualifies as a refugee under Article One
of the nineteen fifty-one UN Convention.

Silence.

YOUNG WOMAN:
I am now left to persuade them that there are human or
compassionate reasons why
I should be allowed to remain in England.

Lights change.

Pause.

(*Speaks slowly, carefully.*) On March first nineteen ninety-seven
I gave birth to a baby girl
and it was a happy day

I am a poet.
Why do you smile?

And I would like one day
to write a history
of my people,
of my grandmother,

and her grandfather,
the witch doctor,

whose strong magic

made a hole in the sky
for the bird dead
to fly
back to the living
and the living dead's cries
ever jealous
made the earth
rumble and shake
and uproot every Mamba tree
as far as the eye can see.
Which is a very long way
my grandmother's, grandfather's eyes.

Pause.

Nervous, she licks her lips.

(*As if answering.*) Stick to the facts!

You're right
the old tales
distract.

Could I have a glass of
water please?

Don't expect dates,
times,
places
or names

My husband's family
are still there,
and my two brothers.
God help them,
not your God

And walls have ears.
Can I have a glass of water
please?

Pause.

I will tell you my story
some bits you won't believe.

Here and there, a day, a week
goes missing
sometimes the pictures shiver,
and the voices shriek,
in my head.
sometimes they shred.

Pause.

Of course, simply.

Pause.

Thank you.
Forget I'm black
by the way
I could be pink
or puce
or grey

English tap water
smells like piss.
Don't they complain
the English?

(*Firmer.*) As I say
March first was a happy day

For three whole weeks
my husband was home
from University

47

He has
his grandmother's
grandfather's eyes
and a big laugh,
he had...

My mother father
and younger sister
Abo stayed home
to see me through
the birth
of my first child.

My mother
was a housewife.
She cooked
and cleaned.
She loved to sing
rock and roll
you understand.
She was clever
with her hands,
she had crocheted
a white wool shawl
threaded with lace ribbon.

My father worked
for the water board.

My sister worked
in a shop
waiting to go to
a London art college
to study
fashion drawing.

She was a talented artist.
as I said
I am a poet

but

to make ends meet
while my husband studied

I worked as a journalist
for eight and a half months
three days a week.
On February ninth
I received a note
posted to the office
where I worked.

It wasn't signed.
I wasn't scared.

Journalists
who wrote
on issues
concerning
human rights

routinely
received threats

but

words are bullets
And one day
from me
perhaps
a careless spray.

A careless spray.

As I say
March first nineteen ninety-seven
was a happy day!

This is what happened
on March second.

YOUNG WOMAN is breathless; sometimes emotion threatens to overwhelm her.

Screams and sounds of chaos.

YOUNG WOMAN AS SOLDIERS:
BITCH CUNT!
YOU BITCH CUNT!
YOU BITCH CUNT!

YOUNG WOMAN:
Soldiers were they?

My sister at the table
a copy of last months Vogue
got from the shop.

She is drawing
the seasons dresses,
colouring them in
with a kids pencil crayon set.

Red being the year's black.

Just before,
they kicked in the door

and shot off her face,

because they hadn't liked
the words I'd written

she smudged one line
with a small wet finger,
excited,
at getting it
exactly right.

She screams.

No No No. Not her, not her!
No, Me! ME! ME!

YOUNG WOMAN AS HUSBAND:
> Get back! Keep back!
> Get under! Stay under!

YOUNG WOMAN:
> My husband
> in front of me
> stopped the bullets
> for a while
> then died I think,
> without a sound.

> *YOUNG WOMAN, as her mother, wails uncontrollably.*

> (*Suddenly calm.*) He was a son to her.
> Smaller than hers,
> and sweeter tempered
> but a son.

> My father springs
> he speaks in tongues.

> His madness makes them stop.
> And –
> for just a half second,
> of a second,
> their jaws drop.

> Strong magic
> has made him
> three men's height
> and strength.
> Then
> they plunge their bayonets
> in him,
> without hate
> it seems,
> the swift jabs
> and light steps

as delicate
and dainty
as a dance.

The tall one's
bayonet

pierces the linoleum,
sticks in
and breaks.

He curses

YOUNG WOMAN AS SOLDIERS:
You fucking old man cunt
Now look what you done!

YOUNG WOMAN:
Pulling it out of my father's neck
he tries to fix it back
on his rifle.
He can't.
He seems put out.

A single bullet
through one eye
stops the horror
for my mother.

*YOUNG WOMAN starts to edge back panting, whimpering.
She is terrified.*

The mewl of the new born baby.

YOUNG WOMAN:
(*Very softly.*) My baby,
oh my baby,
please, please,
my baby, my baby...

The tall one
whose bayonet is broken

takes a machete
from his side

She fixes her arm tight, to keep the baby in her arms.

He grins.
He has a gold tooth
and a diamond stud.

She drops her arm, as if the baby has been snatched from her.

And shouts
and slavers
like an old bull.

They watch

They watch.

My baby, my baby. My baby.

Silence.

Anele
One day
and a million years old.

The bird dead
will come down
through the hole in the sky
and carry your small spirit.
back to our people in the clouds,

And the living dead
ever jealous
will make the earth
rumble and shake
and uproot every mamba tree

as far as the eye can see
which is a very long way
my grandmothers, grandfathers eye.

She is whimpering.

Pause.

(*Broken.*) Please kill me.

Lights change, brighter.

YOUNG WOMAN AS CAMPSFIELD OFFICIAL:
So you want to die?

YOUNG WOMAN:
No I want to be free and live.

(*Calmly.*) I am on hunger strike.

I am waiting for the result of my appeal
I am waiting to receive
Exceptional Leave to Remain.
To be free of fear
for myself.
I will never lose
the fear for my friends,
or the pain.

YOUNG WOMAN AS DOCTOR:
Do you know anything about
force feeding?

No?

It's a fairly horrid business.
A small tube
is forced down
the patient's throat
or sometimes the nose,
sometimes the patient
can be sedated,
but not always!
The whole business
is extremely undignified
unpleasant

and
uncomfortable
for everyone.

You don't believe me?

YOUNG WOMAN:
I believe anything.

Lights change.

John Radcliffe Hospital,
Headington
June nineteen ninety-seven

I weigh six and a half stone

*Two NURSES are making the bed around the drugged
YOUNG WOMAN.*

They whisper.

YOUNG WOMAN AS FIRST NURSE:
A multi gym,
with step treads
and overheads,
a pool
a library

cafeteria
and a snooker room,
ping pong!
It's all wrong if you ask me.
I mean
they run these detention centres
like 18 – 30 clubs

YOUNG WOMAN AS SECOND NURSE:
(*Gently.*) Watch it
you'll give her
blanket burn
you dozy bitch

YOUNG WOMAN AS FIRST NURSE:
> Then there's you and me Elaine
> saving up our coppers
> for a couple of weeks
> backend in Spain.

YOUNG WOMAN AS SECOND NURSE:
> Her tongue's
> all swollen
> look
> poor cow.
> You'd think somehow
> Admissions
> might have mentioned this,
> made a note
> somewhere.
> They're putting a tube
> down there
> tomorrow

YOUNG WOMAN AS FIRST NURSE:
> What I don't understand
> if it's so bad
> they want to die...
>
> Why don't they
> just go back
> to their own country?

YOUNG WOMAN AS SECOND NURSE:
> Sssh.
> Sister'll
> hear you!

YOUNG WOMAN AS FIRST NURSE:
> I reckon
> they should
> send her packing too

(Much, louder.) They're you're done
you naughty girl

YOUNG WOMAN:
(To audience.) I wet the bed

YOUNG WOMAN AS SECOND NURSE:
Next time
press the button see.
It's not too hard
to remember
Eh?

We can't be
changing sheets
every two minutes
for you,
when there's
real sick people
to see to.

Pause.

Lights change.

YOUNG WOMAN:
(Surprised, weakly.) Mr Pennington!

(To audience.) My solicitor,
utterly transformed

in a crumpled
pink and green
Hawaiian shirt

YOUNG WOMAN AS SOLICITOR:
(Very kind.) Young lady
goodness me
I'd no idea

YOUNG WOMAN:
> I last saw him
> four and a half weeks ago.
> He dazzles.

YOUNG WOMAN AS SOLICITOR:
> The shirt
> is dreadful
> isn't it?

> It's the last
> clean something
> in the drawer

> Dear, dear

> Seeing you
> is so distressing.
> I knew of course
> about your fast.
> A bit of good news
> at last

YOUNG WOMAN:
> (*To audience.*) The result of my appeal?

YOUNG WOMAN AS SOLICITOR:
> The names
> you gave
> have come
> up trumps

> one of the
> British journalists
> on assignment in 'ninety-six
> got back to me
> and is prepared
> to substantiate
> your story

YOUNG WOMAN:
  (*Flatly.*) My story?

YOUNG WOMAN AS SOLICITOR:
  That articles
  written by you
  in the political
  climate of the time
  would have been
  interpreted
  as highly inflammatory

  Of course…

YOUNG WOMAN:
  I start to cry

YOUNG WOMAN AS SOLICITOR:
  I don't want
  to get your hopes too high
  but I'll try and get
  this in front of
  the Special Adjudicator
  A.S.A.P.

YOUNG WOMAN:
  Fat tears
  splash
  onto
  the
  sharp
  white
  shroud
  they
  dressed
  me
  up
  in.

YOUNG WOMAN AS SOLICITOR:
(*Very kind, embarrassed.*) Dear girl,
we can't have this

(*Suddenly.*) and you must eat.

Now.
Right away

I'll call
the nurse.

You'll need
your strength

for all
that lies
ahead.

YOUNG WOMAN:
I thank Mr Pennington
For the one hundred and forty two
letters
he has written
so far
on my behalf,

and four and a half hours
of phone calls.

I politely inquire
after his good wife.

YOUNG WOMAN AS SOLICITOR:
She died
my dear.

At two a.m.
last night
she died

Lights dim.

YOUNG WOMAN:
>Campsfield.

>I eat
>a perfect yellow plum
>it would bruise
>to my thumb.

>The miraculous juice
>drips
>sticky and sweet.
>My first solid food
>in twenty-eight days.

>I wipe my hands
>and take a sheet
>of creamy paper.
>And I write,
>slow and shaking
>to the hospital Administrator,
>complaining
>of the remarks
>made by two nurses
>believing me to be asleep.
>The words;
>so long
>locked up,
>are
>dry and hard,
>like
>shrivelled nuts.
>I roll
>them between
>thumb and forefinger
>in the warm damp
>palms of my hand.

>*Lights change.*

YOUNG WOMAN AS THE GAMBIAN:
Right!
Now look here
you

YOUNG WOMAN:
The Gambian,
this is his
fourth complaint
about the food.

YOUNG WOMAN AS THE GAMBIAN:
(*Stroppy.*) We have had it confirmed,
that the beef burgers
served of late
on Friday
and Monday last
were all
well out of date,
and consequently
would explain
the spate
of recent
gastronomic illnesses
stomach pain
and vomiting
amongst inmates
I therefore request this be –

YOUNG WOMAN AS GUARD:
No!

YOUNG WOMAN AS THE GAMBIAN:
brought to the –

YOUNG WOMAN AS GUARD:
No!
No!
Do you hear me?
No!

Lights change.

YOUNG WOMAN:
August twentieth nineteen ninety-seven

Dawn
breaks
like
glass

YOUNG WOMAN AS WARDER:
Come on
wakey, wakey
rise and shit.
You're on your billy bike
to serious clink.

YOUNG WOMAN:
Following his
complaint
about the food
the day before,

the Gambian
is being
"bumped out"

forcibly removed
to Winston Green
or
Rochester
or
Reading gaol

on some
trumped up
charge,

ill discipline
or
lack of co-operation

or
simply
usually
"too much fat lip"

If proved
these accusations
bring
instant
deportation.

YOUNG WOMAN AS STRUGGLING YOUNG MAN:
(*Screaming.*) Not my neck.
No
Not my neck
Not my...

YOUNG WOMAN AS FIRST FEMALE DETAINEE:
They're strangling him!

YOUNG WOMAN AS SECOND FEMALE DETAINEE:
You're strangling him man
oh no

You're killing him!

They're killing him
see man
he's gonna die!
he's gonna die!

YOUNG WOMAN:
The boy
sucks at the air
to try
to make screams

YOUNG WOMAN AS FIRST FEMALE DETAINEE:
He's turning blue
I tell you

he's turning…
he's turning…

YOUNG WOMAN:
He panics
lashing out.

YOUNG WOMAN AS GUARD:
Temper.
Temper.

YOUNG WOMAN:
They pin him
to the ground
his chin an inch
from their feet.

YOUNG WOMAN AS GUARD:
Don't piss about
or we'll make burgers
out of you,
black meat.

Tape: running footsteps.

YOUNG WOMAN:
Reinforcements
arrive
grinning.

Too many men
for one
small struggling boy.

The scuffle
shifts
the dust.

Onlookers gather
and stamp
and rumble,

words
get spat.

YOUNG WOMAN AS ONLOOKERS:
Bullies!

What if that
was your son?

YOUNG WOMAN:
And then
a frustrated guard
with a kind of
slow motion
viciousness
raises his baton
and someone falls.

YOUNG WOMAN, in slow motion puts hands up to her head and in slow motion falls.

African music.

Lights change.

YOUNG WOMAN:
(*As if running fast.*) Come on
not that way
here.

She stops and squats.

wait a minute
get your breath back
wait!

Siren.

YOUNG WOMAN AS FIRST PROTESTER:
Oh Christ
I can smell smoke

YOUNG WOMAN AS SECOND PROTESTER:
(*Wailing.*) No.

YOUNG WOMAN:
The sirens
for the break out,
and that's all

YOUNG WOMAN AS CHILD-MAN:
Look see
Group 4
guards
with sticks
smashing the phones
smashing
smashing

YOUNG WOMAN:
(*Incredulous.*) What are you doing?

YOUNG WOMAN AS GUARD:
We're helping you
that's all

YOUNG WOMAN:
Oh Christ

YOUNG WOMAN AS PROTESTER:
Not that way girl
they're sealing the building
there's no way through.

Out into the library
out into…

YOUNG WOMAN:
Behind the wire
desperation
which makes people mad
now makes torches

YOUNG WOMAN AS GIRL LOCKED IN:
Help, please
we're locked in
the guards locked us in
and the smoke…

God help us.

YOUNG WOMAN AS PROTESTER:
We'll have to break the doors down

They charge the door.

And!
And again!

YOUNG WOMAN:
Come on!
Come on!
Out!
Out!

Lights change.

Out!
Out into the courtyard.

Fifty brothers and sisters
spill
suddenly dangerous
into the mean sunshine

the air smelling like freedom

some will lose their voice
at the injustice of it.

An old man
kicks down a wooden door
finding pots and planks,
and paints
"prisoners of conscience"

pointing his placard
at the cameras

YOUNG WOMAN AS THE OLD MAN:
I had a wife,
a son!
I was a good father
and a hard worker.
I am NOT A CRIMINAL!

LOUDSPEAKERS:
Please leave the courtyard
I repeat
Leave the courtyard

YOUNG WOMAN AS PROTESTER:
Marksmen, see
on their Landrovers
pointing rifles at us

LOUDSPEAKERS:
You are in serious breach of the law

YOUNG WOMAN:
The smoke
curls up to the clouds

LOUDSPEAKERS:
You are surrounded
and outnumbered
your protest is futile
I repeat
your protest…

YOUNG WOMAN:
The smoke
curls up to the English clouds
in thin grey lonely wisps

and I hear someone say
"They'll have to do something now, won't they?"

The sound of the protest peaks.

Pause.

Lights change.

For two days and nights
men and women
old and young
were kept securely
in the visitors centre,

where we slept
on the floor
like dogs.

What do you mean?
participating in the affray?

I saw no participating,

just frightened
people
trying to run away!

I dispute that totally.
In no way
could the protest
be said
to be premeditated,
in no way!

(*Calling out, panic-stricken.*) Why is the door locked?

YOUNG WOMAN AS FELLOW DETAINEE:
You ask too many questions,
girl

YOUNG WOMAN:
You have no right
to lock our doors

Pause.

My file is missing!

(*Panicked.*) my personal case notes –
a blue
lever arch file
four inches thick.

YOUNG WOMAN AS GUARD:
Looted.
in the riot
by your pals.

YOUNG WOMAN:
No! no!
why take my notes,
and leave my bag
and cash?

YOUNG WOMAN AS FELLOW DETAINEE:
You ask too many…

YOUNG WOMAN:
I wish to go to the toilet

YOUNG WOMAN AS GUARD:
You'll wait

YOUNG WOMAN:
What?

YOUNG WOMAN AS GUARD:
You'll wait
you'll effin' wait

YOUNG WOMAN:
Pardon?

YOUNG WOMAN AS GUARD:
(*Looking at watch.*) Right
you got thirty seconds
that's time
for knickers down

your business
wipe
and knickers up –

I'm counting
leave the door ajar.

YOUNG WOMAN:
This can't be happening
in England, August nineteen ninety-seven.

I must speak
to my solicitor.

YOUNG WOMAN AS GUARD:
Visitors from lawyers
are not permitted.

YOUNG WOMAN:
That is a fundamental breach
of human rights.

YOUNG WOMAN AS GUARD:
Is it?

YOUNG WOMAN:
I wish to phone
my lawyer

YOUNG WOMAN AS GUARD:
No incoming
or outgoing calls
are possible

YOUNG WOMAN:
What?

YOUNG WOMAN AS GUARD:
Your pals
smashed
all the phones

YOUNG WOMAN:
>I am writing it down
>I am keeping a record
>I am writing it...

Sudden lights change.

YOUNG WOMAN adopts legs apart, hands in the air position.

The daily body search
another new rule
since the protest.

Afterwards
we feel dirty.

Stripped off
and in my first shower
for two weeks

the guard,
a peep tom
almost
loses his skin
when I scream.

She screams many times in great distress flailing her arms.

Lights change.

Mr Pennington is taking notes.

I am covered in small scratches
and pinch bruises.

I have lost
two or three
clumps of hair,

blood vessels
have burst in my left eye,
the white
is now red,

and it winks
on its own
like a cheery demon.

YOUNG WOMAN AS SOLICITOR:
(*Very gently.*) But
your injuries
are
self inflicted
yes?

YOUNG WOMAN:
Shame is like a fire.
In the shower
I tore at my own flesh
pulling at my cheek
to rip skin
from bone,

clawing my own breasts,

banging my skull
against the cracked tiles

YOUNG WOMAN AS SOLICITOR:
The guard
denies
spying on you

He was,
he says
simply on duty
in the corridor
adjoined.

The authorities
insist
his rapid
intervention

saved
you from more
serious
self harm.

Are you alright my dear?

Pause.

I've made a note
of your complaints,

I'll draft a letter
later on today.
If as seems possible
human rights
have been violated
since the protest

we'll take
this matter
on from there

Pause.

however,

I will admit
my fears
in pursuing
a higher
profile
for yourself
just now

YOUNG WOMAN:
He has a cleaning lady now
Rina
A Filipini
who sows on
all his buttons

and puts knife creases
in his pants

YOUNG WOMAN AS SOLICITOR:
This New Labour Government
are looking for scalps
to hang
on the Home Office belt.

While we wait
for the result
of your appeal,

my advice
to you
young lady
is to live
a quiet life.

Tape: 'The Archers' theme tune.

YOUNG WOMAN:
I have been
removed
to Tinsley house.
a detention centre
for asylum seekers
near Gatwick
run by the American Company
Wackenhut
their ethos
famously
non-confrontational

YOUNG WOMAN sings African tribal song simple, beautiful.

YOUNG WOMAN AS JANICE:
(*Leading applause. London accent.*) Thank you.
That was beautiful
I'm sure, like myself,

everyone here
feels
that you were singing
not just for yourself,
but
for dispossessed people
everywhere.

YOUNG WOMAN:
Tinsley's like
a modern hotel
except each room
looks in on others
like itself

YOUNG WOMAN AS JANICE:
And Elsie
the drop scones
were delicious
as always

YOUNG WOMAN:
Only in the visitors room
can you see the world
sky and the planes
and the busy main road.

(*To audience.*) My friends
were paying
my legal fees

the money
has now
run out.
The surprising
Mr Pennington,
acts for me

She thinks.

altruistically.

YOUNG WOMAN AS MARY:
My
you is lucky girl
most of the suits

charge a tenner
for the spit
on a stamp.

YOUNG WOMAN:
During the protest
Group 4
allege paper work
pertaining to detainees'
cases
has been lost
or destroyed,

and this has
resulted in delays
to hundreds of appeals

including mine.

YOUNG WOMAN AS MARY:
What use
you sweating
on it then?

YOUNG WOMAN:
Mary,
my room mate
is a Pentecostal Christian.
She came over for her cousin's wedding,
met a man,
fell in love
and just
didn't go home

YOUNG WOMAN AS MARY:
>No one
>and nothing
>for me there.

YOUNG WOMAN:
>She has
>a nine month baby

YOUNG WOMAN AS MARY:
>See another card
>from the church
>wishing me well
>God is good.

YOUNG WOMAN:
>I've nothing
>against him
>you understand,
>but her God
>is not mine

>*Lights change.*

>The days
>are like snails,

>Sundays
>are the slowest.

>About midday
>time stops
>altogether
>with a thud,

>screws
>tighten
>in my skull

>my palms itch
>my finger prickle

and
my legs jiggle,

so that I have to keep
stamping my feet.

My minds
on elastic then.

Stretching
all the way
home

and I smell
Sundays,
sweet potatoes
onion bread,

and then burning,
and then
only smoke.

YOUNG WOMAN AS DOCTOR:
(Referring to case notes, she speaks briskly.)
Apart from a brief appearance
in a
Wednesday afternoon
stand and show
attempts at social interaction
now
are nil.

She stays
in her room
looking at the
four walls
all day.

She's highly intelligent
ferociously articulate

manipulative
in her answers,

and has a lot of anger.

To grant her
temporary admission
on the grounds
of sickness,
mental or physical,
would I believe
open the floodgates
to her many fellows,

most of whom
might be said
to be suffering
from depression
claustrophobia
skin disorders
and the rest.

Absconding
is in my opinion,
a real risk

I have prescribed
paracetamol
for the headache,
an anti-fungal
for the hands

My advice
to you
is to refuse
T.A.
on medical grounds

and my advice
to her,

is to join
one of your many
clubs

Lights change.

YOUNG WOMAN AS SOLICITOR:
(*Very gentle, concerned.*) The food is good?

YOUNG WOMAN nods her head.

YOUNG WOMAN:
You have access
to books,
newspapers,
writing materials
and so on?

YOUNG WOMAN nods again.

YOUNG WOMAN AS SOLICITOR:
The exercise classes
are excellent
I believe.

And…
the people
are kind here
yes?

The guards?

YOUNG WOMAN:
(*Very softly.*) Yes
they are kind.

(*To audience.*) Mr Pennington
has reinvented
himself
in a smart jade shirt
and matching tie.
He takes a deep breath.

YOUNG WOMAN AS SOLICITOR:
> I am very
> sorry indeed
> to have to tell you
> your appeal
> has unfortunately
> been dismissed
> by the Special Adjudicator.
> However...

YOUNG WOMAN:
> Overhead
> a plane smothers
> his words,
>
> and I see myself
> in the clouds
> flying home

YOUNG WOMAN AS SOLICITOR:
> So the next step
> is to take the case forward
> to a
> Special Appeal Tribunal.
>
> Make no mistake,
> we've a few tricks
> up our sleeve
> before we
> throw in
> the towel...
>
> roll over
> and...
> er
> die.

YOUNG WOMAN:
> We laugh
>
> Why not?

YOUNG WOMAN AS SOLICITOR:
(*Smiling, relieved.*) Now,
on a less urgent
matter,

I have received
a reply
to your
complaints
regarding
ill treatment
after the protest.

YOUNG WOMAN:
I hardly listen

We were never denied access to lawyers –
a misunderstanding
it seems,

not locked in –
but confined,
the meagre
portions
of food
were not
deliberate policy

but
staff vindictiveness
disciplined
and sorted,

toilet paper
was never rationed,

showers timed!

Body searches
are an essential
security measure.

There has never been
any verbal racist abuse
or
sexual harassment
of female detainees!

YOUNG WOMAN AS SOLICITOR:
I don't believe
a word they say
but in the face
of blunt denial
supported from the very top,
that is the Home Office,
it'll be hard
to make your charges
stick,

if not impossible.
I'm sorry

YOUNG WOMAN:
(*Softly.*) Thanks
anyway.

YOUNG WOMAN AS SOLICITOR:
And there is
more news
you'll find
upsetting
I am sure

YOUNG WOMAN:
On the fourteenth November
nine black men
including my friend
the child man,
were charged
with violent disorder
and riot
following the Campsfield protest

Lights dim.

Against Mr Pennington's advice
I am writing to my young friend
who is in Reading Young Offenders' Institute
to volunteer myself
as a possible defence witness
for him
and others.

African music.

I have kick-started
time again.

The ferocious days
dance now.

YOUNG WOMAN AS MARY:
(*Seated making paper chains.*) Derek will bring
Larrington on Christmas Eve
and we'll open
all his presents
here together

YOUNG WOMAN:
She is making miles
of paper chains,
enough to reach
Jamaica and back.

YOUNG WOMAN AS MARY:
We'll make
the visitors room
as pretty
as we can.

YOUNG WOMAN:
She licks
and coils
and sticks,

the chains
fall in heavy loops
round her black
bare feet.

YOUNG WOMAN AS MARY:
Course he's too small
now
to know a thing

but

She laughs.

Derek says him
loves to sing

waves his little fists
and coos
Derek says

YOUNG WOMAN:
Then
out of a box
she takes a
baby shawl

YOUNG WOMAN AS MARY:
See this fine thing!
One of the old ladies
I clean for
made it
for my baby boy

YOUNG WOMAN:
From white spit
and silver hair
and ivory years

YOUNG WOMAN AS MARY:
The kindness
of folk

shines out
at Christmas

shines out

Pause.

You alright darling?

Pause.

You alright?

Pause.

YOUNG WOMAN:
Yes I'm alright

Lights change.

YOUNG WOMAN AS INTERROGATOR:
And then they shot
your father is it?

YOUNG WOMAN:
No!
no!
my husband.

YOUNG WOMAN AS INTERROGATOR:
With a single shot?

YOUNG WOMAN:
No
they were spraying
bullets everywhere
by then

YOUNG WOMAN AS INTERROGATOR:
Really?
And yet you yourself
escaped
all those bullets?

YOUNG WOMAN:
(*Halting.*) I was lower down
on a day bed,
I don't think
they'd seen me then

and…
my husband…

YOUNG WOMAN AS INTERROGATOR:
Acted as a shield,
yes thank you.
Now they killed
your father
with a bayonet

am I right?

YOUNG WOMAN:
Yes

YOUNG WOMAN AS INTERROGATOR:
How extraordinary.
Why take the trouble
of suddenly bayoneting
someone
when you're in the middle
of spraying bullets
from your rifle.

YOUNG WOMAN:
They'd stopped shooting

YOUNG WOMAN AS INTERROGATOR:
Really?

YOUNG WOMAN:
Yes

YOUNG WOMAN AS INTERROGATOR:
And had the men
seen you yet?

YOUNG WOMAN:
   I…

YOUNG WOMAN AS INTERROGATOR:
   Yes?

YOUNG WOMAN: I…
   I don't know

YOUNG WOMAN AS INTERROGATOR:
   Well, was it
   a very large room
   you were in?

YOUNG WOMAN:
   Not very large

YOUNG WOMAN AS INTERROGATOR:
   It was morning,
   presumably there was light?

YOUNG WOMAN:
   Yes

YOUNG WOMAN AS INTERROGATOR:
   So
   why hadn't
   they seen
   you?

YOUNG WOMAN:
   I…

YOUNG WOMAN AS INTERROGATOR:
   Yes…?

YOUNG WOMAN:
   I was partially hidden
   behind a curtain.

YOUNG WOMAN AS INTERROGATOR:
   A curtain?

Why didn't you mention
this before?

YOUNG WOMAN:
I...
I forgot
I didn't think
it was important.

YOUNG WOMAN AS INTERROGATOR:
So they suddenly
decided to stop shooting,
and bayonet
your father.

YOUNG WOMAN:
He'd screamed
don't you see
and sprang
at them

he surprised them.

YOUNG WOMAN AS INTERROGATOR:
An unarmed elderly man
"surprised"
three strapping youths

YOUNG WOMAN:
He shocked them
so they stopped shooting.

YOUNG WOMAN AS INTERROGATOR:
Where did they
bayonet your father,
on what part of the body?

YOUNG WOMAN:
Every part

YOUNG WOMAN AS INTERROGATOR:
And then
they calmly decided
to put the bayonets away
and shoot your mother?

YOUNG WOMAN:
(*Faltering, in difficulty.*) I…
Yes…

YOUNG WOMAN AS INTERROGATOR:
Then stop shooting again
and bayonet
your baby daughter.

YOUNG WOMAN:
(*Appears to have difficulty breathing.*) I…
I…

YOUNG WOMAN AS INTERROGATOR:
Perhaps
you'd like
to take
a sip
of water?

YOUNG WOMAN:
(*Very softly.*) my baby
wasn't killed
with bayonets,

the taller one

couldn't
get the bayonet
out of my
father's neck,

he killed
my baby
with his machete.

YOUNG WOMAN AS INTERROGATOR:
Now I'm confused

because it says in your notes
you gave birth to a baby
a few weeks later

Pause.

YOUNG WOMAN:
(*Very tense, tearful, distraught.*) I was raped
by the soldiers
I...
miscarried a foetus
in a bucket
while hiding

YOUNG WOMAN AS INTERROGATOR:
Ah yes.
Are you quite sure of this?

YOUNG WOMAN:
(*Hesitant.*) Yes

YOUNG WOMAN AS INTERROGATOR:
I'm no doctor,
and we probably
need expert advice

but isn't it
highly unlikely
that you conceived
the day after
giving birth.

Is it possible?

YOUNG WOMAN:
I...

YOUNG WOMAN AS INTERROGATOR:
Or is it in fact a medical impossibility!

YOUNG WOMAN:
I…

YOUNG WOMAN AS INTERROGATOR:
You still insist you saw this
grinning foetus
in a bucket?

YOUNG WOMAN:
I…
yes…no…

YOUNG WOMAN AS INTERROGATOR:
Well did you or didn't you?

YOUNG WOMAN:
I…perhaps…I

YOUNG WOMAN AS INTERROGATOR:
I would suggest
you are lying

YOUNG WOMAN:
I…

YOUNG WOMAN AS INTERROGATOR:
I would suggest
you are lying

YOUNG WOMAN:
I…

YOUNG WOMAN AS INTERROGATOR:
I would suggest
your whole story,
the killing of your family
the rape
is nothing
but a pack
of well-schemed lies.

YOUNG WOMAN:
>> (*Almost shouting.*) I am not lying

Pause.

YOUNG WOMAN AS INTERROGATOR:
>> Right
>> well, …
>> can we now clarify
>> when they actually
>> did see you
>> for the first time
>> in the room

YOUNG WOMAN:
>> I don't think
>> it was until
>> my mother was shot.

YOUNG WOMAN AS INTERROGATOR:
>> And yet
>> you presumably
>> hadn't stayed
>> silent all this time,
>>
>> or had you?

YOUNG WOMAN:
>> No!
>> No!
>> I
>> I don't know
>> No!
>> I'd been screaming

YOUNG WOMAN AS INTERROGATOR:
>> Well,
>> why didn't they see
>> you,
>> and shoot you,

if as you claim
they'd come
for you?

YOUNG WOMAN:
   I don't know
   why they didn't

YOUNG WOMAN AS INTERROGATOR:
   Did all four men
   rape you?

YOUNG WOMAN:
   Three
   there were
   three men

YOUNG WOMAN AS INTERROGATOR:
   Did they all rape you?

YOUNG WOMAN:
   Yes

YOUNG WOMAN AS INTERROGATOR:
   And you received injuries
   in this attack?

YOUNG WOMAN:
   Yes?

YOUNG WOMAN AS INTERROGATOR:
   They were…

YOUNG WOMAN:
   A cut lip
   two black eyes
   a broken arm
   and…

YOUNG WOMAN AS INTERROGATOR:
   Yes?

Pause.

You mentioned other injuries
you mentioned
bruising and lacerations
to the anus and vagina

YOUNG WOMAN nods.

Yet when you arrived in England
you showed injuries
consistent with a bar room brawl
no more.

YOUNG WOMAN:
 I had been hiding
 in my country
 for three
 no four weeks

YOUNG WOMAN AS INTERROGATOR:
 What is it?
 three or four.

YOUNG WOMAN:
 I...

YOUNG WOMAN AS INTERROGATOR:
 Why did they rape you?
 And not kill you

Silence.

Tape: African music, a pounding drum.

You see
sadly
we've seen and heard it all
over the years
in these proceedings.

Generally it is reported
that
a woman
in the situation
you describe
from the area
you claim
to come from,
would more likely
be raped
then killed.

Tape: a sudden urgent drumming.

YOUNG WOMAN:
(*Softly, troubled.*) I don't know
why they didn't

YOUNG WOMAN AS INTERROGATOR:
Or
they leave their victims
mutilated

Tape: drumming.

YOUNG WOMAN:
(*To INTERROGATOR.*) I don't know
I…

YOUNG WOMAN AS INTERROGATOR:
And yet
at Heathrow
you did not –
I repeat
not
claim asylum.

In fact
you did not
seek asylum
for a week

YOUNG WOMAN:
I was ill
I was confused

I was…

I was…

I was…

Her words are drowned by final climatic drumming.

Sudden silence.

YOUNG WOMAN AS MARY:
You just tell
the truth darling,

see
that's
Gods shield

that blunts
their poisoned spears.

And look
at it
this way,

they're just
doing their job.

Lights change.

YOUNG WOMAN knocks as if at a door, politely.

YOUNG WOMAN AS FEMALE GUARD:
(*A soft accent, polite.*) Mary,
wake up –
get your things together please.

Mary.

Pause.

Mary.

Anything that won't fit
in your suitcase
put in here

YOUNG WOMAN:
She holds out
a plastic bin liner

YOUNG WOMAN AS MARY:
(*Rising from sleep, confused.*) What?

YOUNG WOMAN AS GUARD:
Would you
like us
to help
you dear?

YOUNG WOMAN AS MARY:
Help?

YOUNG WOMAN AS GUARD:
(*Sympathetically.*) I've brought you coffee
two sugars
cream –
that's right isn't it?
and a round of toast

YOUNG WOMAN AS MARY:
Oh thank you

Slight pause.

YOUNG WOMAN AS GUARD:
No
put something
warmer on for now,
it's bitter cold outside.

YOUNG WOMAN:
What's happening?
Where's she going?

(*To audience.*) Seven weeks ago
Mary received her removal papers
she will be taken
to the airport
then
put on a plane.

(*To GUARD.*) This is ridiculous
you can't deport her,
she has a nine month baby
a husband,
and a home.

Dawn is streaking
a dirty gold

YOUNG WOMAN AS MARY:
It's alright dear,
don't fret now
it's alright,

help me pack
help me...

YOUNG WOMAN:
I press
the anger down,
my feet
are lead.

We put photos
into the suitcase

clothes into the black bin liner.

YOUNG WOMAN AS MARY:
No, no
not this shawl
I was keeping it see,
to hold Larrington
when we were all

back together,
a real family again.

But,
no
give it Derek
will you
will you?

YOUNG WOMAN AS GUARD:
Here let me dear,
let me
do that
for you.

YOUNG WOMAN:
(*Sarcastic.*) oh, that would
be so fucking kind!

YOUNG WOMAN AS MARY:
(*To GUARD.*) She's upset miss
forgive the language
yes,
she's a bit worked up

YOUNG WOMAN:
The morning arrives

I can't
even hear
a bird sing

(*To MARY.*) Goodbye Mary

YOUNG WOMAN AS MARY:
Don't worry about me
this is God's way

YOUNG WOMAN:
Her god
is not mine.

YOUNG WOMAN AS MARY:
>I'm praying
>you'll soon
>be free

Lights change.

YOUNG WOMAN AS AGNES:
>Took up prison visiting
>in my thirties
>could never find anything
>to do on a Saturday night,
>anyway

YOUNG WOMAN:
>Agnes is a retired
>history teacher,
>and an old campaigner,
>with an ear
>to the ground.

YOUNG WOMAN AS AGNES:
>(*Eating.*) Your young friend
>was prescribed
>anti-depressants,

>hoarded them
>then took them all,

>have another slice
>dear, do.

>It was touch
>and go
>for a while
>but
>I am reliably informed
>he has recovered

>though not sufficiently
>to stand trial
>I'd say

the poor young man
No! No!

YOUNG WOMAN:
Agnes' outrage
is a cool breeze
in overheated
Tinsley House

YOUNG WOMAN AS AGNES:
The good news –
the treatment
of the nine
has brought about
a
Free the Campsfield Nine
campaign

the bad news

this government
are looking
to introduce
an
Asylum and Immigration Bill
to make things even harder
for you dear.

Lights change.

YOUNG WOMAN AS SOLICITOR:
One of the crucial problems
as I see it

YOUNG WOMAN:
Mr Pennington
has a new hair do
very short

he looks
like a Caesar
in a blue suit

YOUNG WOMAN AS SOLICITOR:
Is that they can't decide
if you're a port applicant

YOUNG WOMAN:
The Special Appeal Tribunal
turned down
my application
for asylum

YOUNG WOMAN AS SOLICITOR:
To be fair
the area
with you
is genuinely grey.

YOUNG WOMAN:
He also
has a new smile.

YOUNG WOMAN AS SOLICITOR:
(*Joking.*) Let's face it
it would
have been
so much better
if you'd have arrived
half dead.

YOUNG WOMAN:
And a new friend
Jemima.
She is younger than him
articled
and drives a Porsche.

YOUNG WOMAN AS SOLICITOR:
Lack of positive identification
of the political faction
of the killers
also doesn't help.

YOUNG WOMAN:
I feel like crying

YOUNG WOMAN AS SOLICITOR:
But what's the point of crying
better to stay cheerful
hope and wait

YOUNG WOMAN:
I think if I was to cry
Some of the tears
would be
for the fat English lady
in the pretty hat
who weeded his garden.

YOUNG WOMAN AS SOLICITOR:
Anyway my dear,
it doesn't end here,
not yet.

YOUNG WOMAN:
My case goes forward
to Judicial Review

YOUNG WOMAN AS SOLICITOR:
A bit of news
that may or may not
amuse

Mike O'Brien
immigration officer
for this government
has awarded Group 4
a special
"Investors In People" Award

YOUNG WOMAN starts to laugh – it moves into a kind of hysteria.

YOUNG WOMAN:
>I was not called as a
>defence witness
>in the case
>against the Campsfield Nine
>there was no need.

>Despite fervent support
>from the new Labour Government
>and a phone call
>to local police
>from Mr Jack Straw
>urging them to press charges,

>the court case
>collapsed in seventeen days.
>The Judge directed the jury of eight
>white men and four women to give
>a verdict of
>Not Guilty
>which
>it did, with relish.

>My friend
>the child man
>tried to kill
>himself
>twice more.

>*Blackout.*

>*Tape: sound of clicking light switch, repeated.*

YOUNG WOMAN AS AGNES:
>Now is that a fuse
>or just a bulb?

>*A soft strand of light illuminates the stage.*

YOUNG WOMAN:
I smell feet

YOUNG WOMAN AS AGNES:
A bulb,
wait here.

YOUNG WOMAN:
A moonbeam
lights a small bed
made up with clean sheets
and a blanket,

a folded up table,

a glass-fronted cupboard,
a large sagging armchair,

a gas fire,

four weeping walls,

and a window

YOUNG WOMAN heaves, as if trying to open the window.

Tape: the sound of splintering glass.

shit!

She laughs.

YOUNG WOMAN AS AGNES:
(*Breathless as after running up stairs.*) You alright?

(*Seeing broken pane.*) Don't worry
about the broken pane.
It solves
one problem –

the gas fires
are lethal
in these old properties.

At least
I won't be concerned
about you
gassing yourself.

Lights change, stage dimly illuminated.

YOUNG WOMAN:
I have at last been granted
Temporary Admission.

If I break conditions
I can be deported
at any time.

YOUNG WOMAN AS AGNES:
Oh dear
it does
look grim.

YOUNG WOMAN:
This is Clarissa Marchant's
mothers' house
Agnes's friend

YOUNG WOMAN AS AGNES:
All the room are empty now,
she can't sell it
because of Mr Doughty
on the ground floor,
but I've stayed
in this room
myself
over the years,

when it's been
too late
to get back
after the opera.

YOUNG WOMAN:
I was only granted
Temporary Admission
because I had
an address
to go to.

I cannot
change address
without permission.
I must report weekly
to the police station
and the
Department of Social Services
to receive
my thirty pound food voucher.
Of course,
I cannot work.

YOUNG WOMAN AS AGNES:
(*Rooting out her purse.*) My dear,
you must
be kind enough
to let me
help…

YOUNG WOMAN:
I have money
Agnes.

YOUNG WOMAN AS AGNES:
(*Doubtful.*) Yes,
still, I'm sure…

YOUNG WOMAN:
Please
I have enough

(*To audience.*) Two hundred and fifty two pounds
left

YOUNG WOMAN AS AGNES:
You'll need
to show them these

YOUNG WOMAN:
Keys.
like bells.

YOUNG WOMAN AS AGNES:
The old fellow
downstairs
is harmless
but keep
your door locked
just the same

(*Looks at watch.*) now,
I really must…

YOUNG WOMAN:
Agnes cares
for her ninety eight year old mother

Thank you.
thank you

Lights change.

Thank you!

I walk everywhere.

Trafalgar Square…

Shoreditch…
Pudding Lane…
Bloomsbury…

London Bridge.

Sitting in a café
in Covent Garden,
which isn't a garden

I watch the carnival.

A clown on stilts
juggles a plate on a stick
threatening to goo
the gathering crowd.

A statue
suddenly tickles
a tots tum.

A boy
with green hair
offers me a leaflet,
asking
where's God?

And there's the jangle
of knives and cups.

At home
as long as they are remembered
we set a place
and serve food and drink
to dead
loved ones.

I take five
slow sips
of the milky froth

She sips under breath.

for mother...

She sips.

father...

She sips.

Abo...

She sips.

Yemi…

Again she sips but cannot voice the word, finally she mouths:

Anele

YOUNG WOMAN AS YOUNG MAN IN CAFÉ:
(*Loudly.*) Could you pass the pepper please?

> She used to dip her nipples
> in honey
> and then
> porridge oats
> and make me lick my breakfast
> off

YOUNG WOMAN AS OLDER WOMAN:
> Poor Poppy was sick every Monday
> for the whole first term
> so Caroline sent her
> to the lower school shrink.

YOUNG WOMAN:
> The clown juggles wine bottles
> I juggle figures.

> with two hundred and fifty pounds left,
> and six months
> before I can work,
> apart from food vouches
> I must live on
> ten pounds a week.
> Today, already
> I have spent
> seven pounds fifty-five pence.

> I leave,
> taking packets of sugar,
> the teaspoon
> and three napkins.

As the young man and woman leave
I pocket
their leftover
egg and cress roll.

At night
to save heat
and light

I burrow
fully clothed
into blankety blackness,

my warm breath
makes the damp bed
steam.

A knock.

Pause.

Knock again.

Pause.

Who is it?

YOUNG WOMAN AS MR DOUGHTY:
(*Irish.*) I'm Mr Doughty
I live downstairs

(*As if to edge the door open.*) Doesn't the light work?

YOUNG WOMAN:
Yes

He switches the light on.

YOUNG WOMAN AS MR DOUGHTY:
I'm sorry dear
I didn't think…

YOUNG WOMAN:
> No…
> please

YOUNG WOMAN AS MR DOUGHTY:
> I've brought you this

YOUNG WOMAN:
> (*She inhales.*) Home made
> vegetable soup
> steaming
> in fragrant curly wisps!

YOUNG WOMAN AS MR DOUGHTY:
> Brass monkeys
> in here
> dear.

YOUNG WOMAN:
> I eat the soup
> downstairs
> in Mr Doughty's
> red-hot kitchen.
>
> He tells me
> of his
> forty-year struggle
>
> against British Imperialism.
>
> And we watch
> together on his
> black and white TV
>
> a wildlife programme
>
> on seals.

Lights change.

Tape: bleeping sound, items going through checkout at a supermarket.

YOUNG WOMAN AS CHECK OUT GIRL:
No, sorry.

YOUNG WOMAN:
Pardon?

YOUNG WOMAN AS CHECK OUT GIRL:
You can't have these

YOUNG WOMAN:
(*Embarrassed.*) I…

YOUNG WOMAN AS CHECK OUT GIRL:
(*Slowly and loudly as to a foreigner.*) Your vouchers are for food
alright?
comprenez?
things you put in your gob?
chew –
come out the other end.

you can't eat sanitary towels!

well I suppose
you could
with a bit of marmite
on them.

She laughs.

Lights change.

YOUNG WOMAN:
Mr Pennington
calls me
on the communal phone

YOUNG WOMAN AS MR DOUGHTY:
It's himself
is it?

YOUNG WOMAN:
I squat

on the bottom stair
Mr Doughty
brings a rug

(*Into phone.*) No, the mail's reliable
I received the papers yes

(*To audience.*) in the background, a party

(*Into phone.*) and the date's fine
well
I'm not sure what it could
clash with.
I'm managing thank you

(*To audience.*) I have one hundred and thirty two pounds
fifty-seven pence left.

Through the popping champagne corks
and laughter
I hear

YOUNG WOMAN AS JEMIMA:
(*To MR PENNINGTON.*) Eddy…
darling…
darling look…

YOUNG WOMAN:
(*Back into phone.*) Freedom?
it's wonderful

Lights change.

Night after night
I sit
in Mr Doughty's kitchen

we take turns
to cook
in time
for the six o'clock news

One night
we watch British planes
bombard Belgrade

YOUNG WOMAN AS MR DOUGHTY:
Too much salt
in the fish soup
you reckon?

YOUNG WOMAN:
There are Kosovans
in Campsfield
I'm sure of it

YOUNG WOMAN AS MR DOUGHTY:
Not for long
I'd say.
Dip your bread in
mop up the last
little bit.

Lights change.

YOUNG WOMAN AS CLARISSA MARCHANT:
(*Extremely upper class.*) I'm sorry dear,
I really am.

YOUNG WOMAN:
Clarissa Marchant,
her mother
owns the house.

YOUNG WOMAN AS CLARISSA MARCHANT:
But you have to admit
you've had a good innings

YOUNG WOMAN:
After nearly five months
I have been told
to leave
by Friday

YOUNG WOMAN AS CLARISSA MARCHANT:
Of course I said
they could have
the whole house.

Well I am chair
of the committee.

We've all been
so moved
by their plight,
who could fail
to be?

But
it's not up to scratch
apparently,
the house

She snorts with laughter.

not "sanitary"
or some such nonsense!
You'd think
after what
they've been through!

So it's this room
or nothing.

YOUNG WOMAN:
My brain
starts to
fast forward

YOUNG WOMAN AS CLARISSA MARCHANT:
She's been through Hell
poor girl.
Eletia's her name

Pretty isn't it?
from Kosovo herself.

Been incarcerated
in one of those rape centres,
can you imagine?
Doesn't know
where her family are,
speaks
the most charming
broken English

YOUNG WOMAN:
Do I have
to tell Social Security
I've lost my address?
Will they send me back inside?
Yes
if I tell the police.

YOUNG WOMAN AS CLARISSA MARCHANT:
Your business
is on the brink
of sorting out
I've heard.

I'm sure you've made
lots of friends
who'll gladly put you up
pretty girl like you?

YOUNG WOMAN:
I…
well…

YOUNG WOMAN AS CLARISSA MARCHANT:
(*Dismissive.*) Anyway dear
I've told them
now

(*Looking around.*) somebody mentioned
the press might want a photo.

Oh dear,
it's pretty grim up here,

a couple of cheap rugs
would cheer it up,

a duvet

and new curtains perhaps.

She sees broken window pane.

(*Sternly.*) What's this?

YOUNG WOMAN:
I'm sorry
I broke the pane,
opening the window

YOUNG WOMAN AS CLARISSA MARCHANT:
Well
you'll pay for it.

YOUNG WOMAN:
Pay?

YOUNG WOMAN AS CLARISSA MARCHANT:
Yes!
I mean
I've let you stay
rent free,
I'm damned
if I'll pay
for your breakages.

YOUNG WOMAN:
Right.

YOUNG WOMAN AS CLARISSA MARCHANT:
Twenty pounds will do

YOUNG WOMAN:
(*Horrified.*) Twenty pounds
I…

YOUNG WOMAN AS CLARISSA MARCHANT:
Oh
a tenner then.

YOUNG WOMAN:
(*To audience.*) I have
fifty-five pounds ninety pence left.

YOUNG WOMAN AS CLARISSA MARCHANT:
Oh,
and you'll
wash the sheets
before you go?

Lights change.

Knocking.

YOUNG WOMAN AS MR DOUGHTY:
What's the matter dear?
Have I offended you at all?

Pause.

YOUNG WOMAN:
(*Softly.*) No…
I…
I'm not well

YOUNG WOMAN AS MR DOUGHTY:
Well let me in
p'raps I can help.

YOUNG WOMAN:
No
really
I…
I need to be alone.

YOUNG WOMAN AS MR DOUGHTY:
I've a rhubarb crumble
I baked
last night

Pause.

Come down dear
warm yourself.

YOUNG WOMAN:
Really I…

Pause.

(*Loudly.*) Please
just leave me alone.

YOUNG WOMAN AS MR DOUGHTY:
(*Sadly.*) Getting too attached
was I?
I'm sorry,
people think
when you're old
you don't have those feelings
but you do.

Ridiculous.

You're a beautiful young woman,
a princess.

I'm just a broken down
old fool

Pause.

I'd never have
laid a finger on you

never.

Lights change.

African music.

YOUNG WOMAN packs her bag.

YOUNG WOMAN:
Friday morning
before he wakes

I slip a note
under his door
it reads

thank you for your friendship.

Lights change.

Tape: London traffic.

YOUNG WOMAN AS YOUTH:
(*He has a slight speech impediment.*) You're not waiting
for a bus
are you?

Pause.

YOUNG WOMAN:
Friday evening
ten to ten

YOUNG WOMAN AS YOUTH:
How do I know?

Pause.

I've been carefully watching you.

Every single bus
has been and gone
and you're still here.

YOUNG WOMAN:
Very clever

Pause.

YOUNG WOMAN AS YOUTH:
Your old man
kicked you out
did he?

YOUNG WOMAN:
(*Cautiously, weighing him up.*) Yes
that's right,
he'll get over it, of course
in the morning

YOUNG WOMAN AS YOUTH:
Of course

YOUNG WOMAN:
But meanwhile…

Pause.

YOUNG WOMAN AS YOUTH:
You can't come home
with me.

YOUNG WOMAN:
No?

YOUNG WOMAN AS YOUTH:
My mum
doesn't like
me bringing
girls back.

I have to do it
up the alley,
back of the launderette.

YOUNG WOMAN:
Really?

YOUNG MAN:
    But I know
    somewhere
    you can go

Lights change.

YOUNG WOMAN AS GUEST HOUSE WOMAN:
    Well?

YOUNG WOMAN:
    A large woman
    with burns
    to her lip, chin and neck
    shows me the room.

    A cockroach scuttles
    over cracked lino.

YOUNG WOMAN:
    How much?

YOUNG WOMAN AS GUEST HOUSE WOMAN:
    Fifty quid
    a night.

YOUNG WOMAN:
    (*Making to leave.*) No
    no I'm sorry
    I can't afford that

YOUNG WOMAN AS GUEST HOUSE WOMAN:
    Oh alright,
    thirty,
    don't tell my husband
    he'd murder me.

YOUNG WOMAN:
    I'm afraid it's still too…

YOUNG WOMAN AS GUEST HOUSE WOMAN:
    Twenty then
    'cos

you're a friend
of Stans

YOUNG WOMAN:
Twenty?

Pause.

Alright twenty.

The room is
twelve foot by six,
the electric light
on a push switch
only stays on
for fifteen seconds

the foot of the sink
is broken
and the tap drips.

As I climb into bed
the rubber under-sheet
stiffened with urine
crackles.

In the darkness
I hear the burnt woman
scream,
then a key
turns
in the lock

YOUNG WOMAN AS YOUTH:
Don't be scared
I won't really hurt you
you're pretty

YOUNG WOMAN:
(*Horrified.*) Get out!

YOUNG WOMAN AS YOUTH:
(*Cowering.*) Don't shout
you hurt
my ears.

YOUNG WOMAN:
GET OUT!
GET OUT!
GET OUT!

Lights change.

YOUNG WOMAN AS REFUGEE NIGHT SHELTER
WORKER:
There's no spaces tonight again
I'm sorry.

YOUNG WOMAN AS IRANIAN REFUGEE:
(*Distressed.*) You promised –
you said
next week
come back.

YOUNG WOMAN AS WORKER:
(*To YOUNG WOMAN.*) Please try again tomorrow.

YOUNG WOMAN:
(*Soft, reasoned.*) I thought you encouraged
a weekly turnover
give people a chance,
to get off the streets.

YOUNG WOMAN AS WORKER:
We do
but there's an outbreak
of flu,
it's making things
very difficult

(*She whispers.*) look,
we've allowed

three or four
to stay in
today,

we're a night shelter,
everyone's supposed to be out
by nine am.

If the council
get wind of it
they'll close us down

YOUNG WOMAN AS IRANIAN REFUGEE:
I am an educated man

YOUNG WOMAN AS WORKER:
(*To young woman.*) Please try again tomorrow.

YOUNG WOMAN AS IRANIAN REFUGEE:
In my country
I'm a civil engineer.
Yesterday
I slept in a park,

my coat's
covered in dog shit,

the smell
makes me sick

YOUNG WOMAN AS WORKER:
You go to the day centre?

YOUNG WOMAN:
Yes

YOUNG WOMAN AS IRANIAN REFUGEE:
I politely
asked the fellow
if he'd finished
with *The Times*

was that causing
trouble?

YOUNG WOMAN AS WORKER:
You get soup there?

YOUNG WOMAN AS IRANIAN REFUGEE:
Soup
Ha!
cats' pee soup!

YOUNG WOMAN AS WORKER:
I was talking
to the young lady

YOUNG WOMAN:
Yes, I get soup

YOUNG WOMAN AS WORKER:
You're still getting your vouchers?

YOUNG WOMAN nods.

I'm sorry?

YOUNG WOMAN:
Yes
I'm getting my vouchers

YOUNG WOMAN AS IRANIAN REFUGEE:
I heard it
on the wireless yesterday
for the Kosovans
the voucher system
won't apply

YOUNG WOMAN AS WORKER:
You're on temporary admission?

YOUNG WOMAN:
Yes, I'm on temporary admission

YOUNG WOMAN AS IRANIAN REFUGEE:
> Why give them money
> and not me?
> I lost a brother
> fighting for democracy.

YOUNG WOMAN AS WORKER:
> (*Softly.*) If you want to stay out
> don't let the police know
> you've lost your address.

Lights change.

Tape: traffic.

YOUNG WOMAN on a bus asleep.

YOUNG WOMAN AS CONDUCTOR:
> (*As if shaking violently.*) Oi!
> Wakey, wakey!

YOUNG WOMAN:
> (*Startled.*) What?

YOUNG WOMAN AS CONDUCTOR:
> This is a bus
> not a bleedin'
> mobile dosshouse
>
> Where's your ticket?

YOUNG WOMAN, roots, finds it, hands it over.

> Well, you've overidden
> by seventeen stops
>
> I am therefore
> obliged to implement
> the five pound penalty fare
> on passengers
> found to be travelling

whilst not in possession
of a valid ticket.

He grins.

Pause.

YOUNG WOMAN:
  I can't…
  I haven't…

YOUNG WOMAN AS CONDUCTOR:
  You haven't looked.

YOUNG WOMAN:
  (*Attempting to search.*) I…

YOUNG WOMAN AS CONDUCTOR:
  (*Shifty.*) Well a couple of quid then

YOUNG WOMAN:
  I don't…
  I haven't…

YOUNG WOMAN AS CONDUCTOR:
  Right, name and address…

  *YOUNG WOMAN jumps up as if over the seat, and careers
  down steps.*

  Tape: screeching brakes, the bus jolts.

  *YOUNG WOMAN lurches and falls down painfully, rolling
  over and over.*

YOUNG WOMAN AS GRETA, AN OLD STREET
WOMAN:
  (*Polish accent.*) Where you been?

What you done to your leg?

Where's your bag?

  *YOUNG WOMAN falls to her knees and starts to half wail,
  half sob.*

Don't cry
black girl
you can have
my bag

YOUNG WOMAN:
My family
photos of my family
Abo –
little sister Abo

the shawl –
Anele's shawl

all
I…

She breaks down, she sounds like an animal.

YOUNG WOMAN AS GRETA:
(*Mischievously she holds up a coin.*) Look what I got

(*Pulling coin away.*) You said
you'd get me
Lucozade
with your special voucher
you said

YOUNG WOMAN:
Please

She takes the coin.

I must make
a phone call

YOUNG WOMAN suddenly panics.

the phone number's
in my bag

Agnes… is o, one, two, four, two, no
o, one, two, two, no

She paces about, trying to remember the right phone number.

Tape: ringing phone.

(*On phone.*) Please God
let Agnes be there
please God
please God

Phone keeps on ringing.

My Gods –
the bird women,
the living dead –
swoop and flutter
their great wings
smashing against the glass

YOUNG WOMAN puts phone down, she dials again.

Phone rings.

YOUNG WOMAN AS HOUSE SITTER:
    Yes?

YOUNG WOMAN:
    (*Hardly able to speak.*) Oh, could I speak
    to Mr Pennington please?

YOUNG WOMAN AS HOUSE SITTER:
    I'm afraid he's away

YOUNG WOMAN:
    Away?

YOUNG WOMAN AS HOUSE SITTER:
    Yes,
    he's on his honeymoon
    in the Caribbean

Pause.

who's this?
I can contact him
if it's important

Pause.

Hello?

Hello, are you
still there?

Pause.

Lights change.

Far away African drumming.

A pin spotlight on YOUNG WOMAN's face, she crouches.

YOUNG WOMAN:
You'd think
hunger
would bite the belly
not the brain.

The bird gods
are vultures.

They're everywhere,
in the bins
back of the Burger King,

on the park bench
with the half chewed
Twix.

They're mischievous too,

in the bottle of pop
in the telephone box
that turns out to be piss.

YOUNG WOMAN AS GRETA:
You could beg.

I can't beg,
you have to have
nice clothes to beg,
and a dog.

You have
to be able
to write.

You could beg
'cos you've got
lovely clothes
and sad eyes.

YOUNG WOMAN:
(*Something snaps.*) How can you bear
to go on living?

(*Suddenly vicious.*) You stupid
wasted
crazy…
woman

She starts to laugh and in time this turns to sobs.

and I'll tell you
another funny thing,
time

it's actually moving forward
when it's really moving back

Tape: African drumming.

*YOUNG WOMAN moans and rocks herself, she undoes her
dress and bares a breast as if to feed a baby.*

African drumming stops.

She looks up, as if into the face of someone, her hands fall to her side, her dress still open.

Lights change.

YOUNG WOMAN AS MAN:
How much?

YOUNG WOMAN:
It depends
what you want

YOUNG WOMAN AS MAN:
Up the bum.

YOUNG WOMAN:
Twenty five pounds

YOUNG WOMAN AS MAN:
Funny

YOUNG WOMAN:
Twenty pounds

YOUNG WOMAN AS MAN:
Ten pounds
and I'll be quick
you've got nice tits

and with a condom, right,
one of those extra strong jobbies.
I've got a wife and kids.

African drumming.

Mmm nice!
I like a bit of rump
and black meat's tough
but tasty…

African drums – louder – faster.

Christ
you've a bony arse.

Louder still.

No!
no!
it's no good

Silence.

It's like fucking a corpse.

Lights change.

Tape: telephone ringing tones, then the phone is picked up.

YOUNG WOMAN AS AGNES:
Seven four three, two six one two
Agnes Holroyd speaking

YOUNG WOMAN tries to speak, she cannot.

Hallo?

YOUNG WOMAN tries to speak, her hand shakes, she trembles.

Hallo
who's there?

YOUNG WOMAN tries to speak.

Hallo!
who's this?

(*Getting annoyed.*) Hallo.

YOUNG WOMAN lets the phone fall from her hand.

Lights change.

YOUNG WOMAN AS JUDGE:
Well it seems to me
there's more holes

in the young woman's story
than in a doily

there's absolutely
no evidence
put before me
to suggest
her life is at risk

in fact
in the ever changing
political climate
she might even
be greeted –
a heroine!

it is highly unlikely
she would have been granted
leave to remain,

now it's a straightforward
case of Absconding
whilst on Temporary Admission

we shall put a search order
out for your client
and recommend immediate return
to country of origin

did you hear me?
Mr Pennington
did you hear me?

Lights change.

YOUNG WOMAN:
(*Looking up to someone, softly spoken.*) Yes.
yes. I hear

oh I don't know
a week.

a month.
a year.

Somebody comes
and leaves tuna mayo
sandwiches

rain
I drink rain.

What's that?

that's a police van is it?

(*Sadly.*) yes, alright

not really
you'll have to help
my legs don't work well.

Thanks.

I'm sorry. I smell

yes,
be careful
I'm bleeding.

Lights change.

YOUNG WOMAN AS SOLICITOR:
The young woman
was held
in a strip cell
in Holloway Prison
for six and a half weeks

YOUNG WOMAN:
I am a poet
why do you smile?

words are hot wax
and this poem-play

is a candle I light
for Anele,

YOUNG WOMAN AS SOLICITOR:
Then
she was deported

YOUNG WOMAN:
for my daughter.
For my daughter
freedom.

YOUNG WOMAN AS SOLICITOR:
She was met
at the airport
in her own country
by her loyal friends

who because of her
changed appearance
at first
did not recognise her

YOUNG WOMAN:
Am I still me?

YOUNG WOMAN AS SOLICITOR:
She was not arrested at the airport
and her re-entry into the country
provoked no comment in the papers

she was hidden successfully
moving from safe house
to safe house.

On August fourteenth 2000*
a group of three young men
in part military uniform
burst into the apartment

* Date should be the day after the performance.

where she
and her three friends
were drinking morning coffee

Tape: blast of gunfire then silence.

They were all killed outright.

Lights change, African music.

The End.